# Book 1
# Python Programming
# Professional Made Easy
### BY SAM KEY

# &

# Book 2
# CSS Programming Professional
# Made Easy
### BY SAM KEY

# Book 1
# Python Programming
# Professional Made Easy

By Sam Key

## *Expert Python Programming Language Success in a Day for Any Computer User!*

**Programming Box Set #52: Python Programming Professional Made Easy & CSS Programming Professional Made Easy**

Programming Box Set #52: Python Programming Professional Made
Easy & CSS Programming Professional Made Easy

# Table Of Contents

# Introduction

I want to thank you and congratulate you for purchasing the book, "Python Programming Professional Made Easy: Expert Python Programming Language Success in a Day for Any Computer User!"

This book contains proven steps and strategies on how to program Python in a few days. The lessons ingrained here will serve as an introduction to the Python language and programming to you. With the little things you will learn here, you will still be able to create big programs.

The book is also designed to prepare you for advanced Python lessons. Make sure that you take note of all the pointers included here since they will help you a lot in the future.

Thanks again for purchasing this book. I hope you enjoy it!

# Chapter 1: Introduction to Programming Languages

This short section is dedicated to complete beginners in programming. Knowing all the things included in this chapter will lessen the confusion that you might encounter while learning Python or any programming language.

Computers do not know or cannot do anything by itself. They just appear smart because of the programs installed on them.

## *Computer, Binary, or Machine Language*

You cannot just tell a computer to do something using human language since they can only understand computer language, which is also called machine or binary language. This language only consists of 0's and 1's.

On the other hand, you may not know how to speak or write computer language. Even if you do, it will take you hours before you can tell a computer to do one thing since just one command may consist of hundreds or thousands of 1's and 0's. If you translate one letter in the human alphabet to them, you will get two or three 1's or 0's in return. Just imagine how many 1's and 0's you will need to memorize if you translate a sentence to computer language.

## *Assembly or Low Level Programming Language*

In order to overcome that language barrier, programmers have developed assemblers. Assemblers act as translators between a human and a computer.

However, assemblers cannot comprehend human language. They can only translate binary language to assembly language and vice versa. So, in order to make use of assemblers, programmers need to learn their language, which is also called a low level language.

Unfortunately, assembly language is difficult to learn and memorize. Assembly language consists of words made from mnemonics that only computer experts know. And for one to just make the computer display something to the screen, a programmer needs to type a lot of those words.

## *High Level Programming Language*

Another solution was developed, and that was high level programming languages such as C++, Java, and Python. High level programming languages act as a translator for humans and assembly language or humans to computer language.

Unlike assembly language (or low level language), high level programming languages are easier to understand since they commonly use English words instead of mnemonics. With it, you can also write shorter lines of codes since they already provide commonly used functions that are shortened into one or two keywords.

## Programming Box Set #52: Python Programming Professional Made Easy & CSS Programming Professional Made Easy

If you take one command or method in Python and translate it to assembly language, you will have long lines of codes. If you translate it to computer language, you will have thousands of lines composed of 1's and 0's.

In a nutshell, high level programming languages like Python are just translators for humans and computers to understand each other. In order for computers to do something for humans, they need to talk or instruct them via programming languages.

Many high level languages are available today. Among the rest, Python is one of the easiest languages to learn. In the next chapter, you will learn how to speak and write with Python language for your computer to do your bidding.

# Chapter 2: Getting Prepped Up

On the previous chapter, you have learned the purpose of programming languages. By choosing this book, you have already decided that Python is the language that you want to use to make your programs. In this chapter, your learning of speaking, writing, and using this language starts.

### *You, Python, and Your Computer*

Before you start writing, take a moment to understand the relationship between you, the programming language, and the computer. Imagine that you are a restaurant manager, and you have hired two foreign guys to cook for the restaurant, which is the program you want to create. The diners in your restaurant are the users of your program.

The first guy is the chef who only knows one language that you do not know. He follows recipes to the letter, and he does not care if the recipe includes him jumping off the cliff. That guy is your computer.

The second guy is the chef's personal translator who will translate the language you speak or write, which is Python, to the language the chef knows. This translator is strict and does not tolerate typos in the recipes he translates. If he finds any mistake, he will tell it right to your face, walk away with the chef, and leave things undone.

He also does not care if the recipe tells the chef to run on circles until he dies. That is how they work. This guy is your programming language.

Since it is a hassle to tell them the recipe while they cook, you decided to write a recipe book instead. That will be your program's code that the translator will read to the chef.

### *Installing Python*

You got two things to get to program in Python. First, get the latest release of Python. Go to this website: https://www.python.org/downloads/.

Download Python 3.4.2 or anything newer than that. Install it. Take note of the directory where you will install Python.

Once you are done with the installation, you must get a source code editor. It is recommended that you get Notepad++. If you already have a source code editor, no need to install Notepad++, too. To download Notepad++, go to: http://www.notepad-plus-plus.org/download/v6.6.9.html. Download and install it.

**Programming Box Set #52: Python Programming Professional Made Easy & CSS Programming Professional Made Easy**

## Version 2.x or 3.x

If you have already visited the Python website to download the program, you might have seen that there are two Python versions that you can download. As of this writing, the first version is Python 3.4.2 and the second version is Python 2.7.8.

About that, it is best that you get the latest version, which is version 3.4.2. The latest version or build will be the only one getting updates and fixes. The 2.7.8 was already declared as the final release for the 2.x build.

Beginners should not worry about it. It is recommended that new Python programmers start with 3.x or later before thinking about exploring the older versions of Python.

## Programming and Interactive Mode

Python has two modes. The first one is Programming and the second one is Interactive. You will be using the Interactive mode for the first few chapters of this book. On the other hand, you will be using the Programming mode on the last few chapters.

In Interactive mode, you can play around with Python. You can enter lines of codes on it, and once you press enter, Python will immediately provide a feedback or execute the code you input. To access Python's interactive mode, go to the directory where you installed Python and open the Python application. If you are running on Windows, just open the Run prompt, enter python, and click OK.

In Programming mode, you can test blocks of code in one go. Use a source editor to write the program. Save it as a .py file, and run it as Python program. In Windows, .py files will be automatically associated with Python after you install Python. Due to that, you can just double click the file, and it will run.

# Chapter 3: Statements

A program's code is like a recipe book. A book contains chapters, paragraphs, and sentences. On the other hand, a program's code contains modules, functions, and statements. Modules are like chapters that contain the recipes for a full course meal. Procedures or functions are like paragraphs or sections that contain recipes. Statements are like the sentences or steps in a recipe. To code a program with Python, you must learn how to write statements.

## *Statements*

Statements are the building blocks of your program. Each statement in Python contains one instruction that your computer will follow. In comparison to a sentence, statements are like imperative sentences, which are sentences that are used to issue commands or requests. Unlike sentences, Python, or programming languages in general, has a different syntax or structure.

For example, type the statement below on the interpreter:

**print("Test")**

Press the enter key. The interpreter will move the cursor to the next line and print 'Test' without the single quotes. The command in the sample statement is print. The next part is the details about the command the computer must do. In the example, it is ("test"). If you convert that to English, it is like you are commanding the computer to print the word Test on the program.

Python has many commands and each of them has unique purpose, syntax, and forms. For example, type this and press enter:

**1 + 1**

Python will return an answer, which is 2. The command there is the operator plus sign. The interpreter understood that you wanted to add the two values and told the computer to send the result of the operation.

## *Variables*

As with any recipe, ingredients should be always present. In programming, there will be times that you would want to save some data in case you want to use them later in your program. And there is when variables come in.

Variables are data containers. They are the containers for your ingredients. You can place almost any type of data on them like numbers or text. You can change the value contained by a variable anytime. And you can use them anytime as long as you need them.

To create one, all you need is to think of a name or identifier for the variable and assign or place a value to it. To create and assign a value to variables, follow the example below:

**example1 = 10**

On the left is the variable name. On the right is the value you want to assign to the variable. If you just want to create a variable, you can just assign 0 to the variable to act as a placeholder. In the middle is the assignment operator, which is the equal sign. That operator tells the interpreter that you want him to assign a value, which is on its right, to the name or object on the left.

To check if the variable example1 was created and it stored the value 10 in it, type the variable name on the interpreter and press enter. If you done it correctly, the interpreter will reply with the value of the variable. If not, it will reply with a NameError: name <variable_name> is not defined. It means that no variable with that name was created.

Take note, you cannot just create any name for a variable. You need to follow certain rules to avoid receiving syntax errors when creating them. And they are:

> Variable names should start with an underscore or a letter.
> Variable names must only contain letters, numbers, or underscores.
> Variable names can be one letter long or any length.
> Variable names must not be the same with any commands or reserved keywords in Python.
> Variable names are case sensitive. The variable named example1 is different from the variable named Example1.

As a tip, always use meaningful names for your variables. It will help you remember them easily when you are writing long lines of codes. Also, keep them short and use only one style of naming convention. For example, if you create a variable like thisIsAString make sure that you name your second variable like that too: thisIsTheSecondVariable not this_is_the_second_variable.

You can do a lot of things with variables. You can even assign expressions to them. By the way, expressions are combinations of numbers and/or variables together with operators that can be evaluated by the computer. For example:

**Example1 = 10**

**Example2 = 5 + 19**

**Example3 = Example1 - Example2**

If you check the value of those variables in the interpreter, you will get 10 for Example1, 24 for Example2, and -14 for Example3.

# Chapter 4: Basic Operators – Part 1

As of this moment, you have already seen three operators: assignment (=), addition (+), and subtraction (-) operators. You can use operators to process and manipulate the data and variables you have – just like how chefs cut, dice, and mix their ingredients.

## *Types of Python Operators*

Multiple types of operators exist in Python. They are:

> - **Arithmetic**
> - **Assignment**
> - **Comparison**
> - **Logical**
> - **Membership**
> - **Identity**
> - **Bitwise**

Up to this point, you have witnessed how arithmetic and assignment operators work. During your first few weeks of programming in Python, you will be also using comparison and logical operators aside from arithmetic and assignment operators. You will mostly use membership, identity, and bitwise later when you already advanced your Python programming skills.

As a reference, below is a list of operators under arithmetic and assignment. In the next chapter, comparison and logical will be listed and discussed briefly in preparation for later lessons.

For the examples that the list will use, x will have a value of 13 and y will have a value of 7.

## *Arithmetic*

Arithmetic operators perform mathematical operations on numbers and variables that have numbers stored on them.

> **+ : Addition. Adds the values besides the operator.**

   **z = 13 + 7**

   z's value is equal to 20.

   **- : Subtraction. Subtracts the values besides the operator.**

   **z = x − y**

z's value is equal to 6.

\* : **Multiplication. Multiplies the values besides the operator.**

**z = x \* y**

z's value is equal to 91.

/ : **Division. Divides the values besides the operator.**

**z = x / y**

z's value is equal to 1.8571428571428572.

\*\* : **Exponent. Applies exponential power to the value to the left (base) with the value to the right (exponent).**

**z = x \*\* y**

z's value is equal to 62748517.

// : **Floor Division. Divides the values besides the operator and returns a quotient with removed digits after the decimal point.**

**z = x // y**

z's value is equal to 1.

% : **Modulus. Divides the values besides the operator and returns the remainder instead of the quotient.**

**z = x % y**

z's value is equal to 6.

## *Assignment*

Aside from the equal sign or simple assignment operator, other assignment operators exist. Mostly, they are combinations of arithmetic operators and the simple assignment operator.

They are used as shorthand methods when reassigning a value to a variable that is also included in the expression that will be assigned to it. Using them in your code simplifies and makes your statements clean.

**= : Simple assignment operator. It assigns the value of the expression on its right hand side to the variable to its left hand side.**

$z = x + y * x - y \% x$

z's value is equal to 97.

The following assignment operators work like this: it applies the operation first on the value of the variable on its left and the result of the expression on its right. After that, it assigns the result of the operation to the variable on its left.

**+= : Add and Assign**

$x += y$

x's value is equal to 20. It is equivalent to x = x + y.

**-= : Subtract and Assign**

$x -= y$

x's value is equal to 6. It is equivalent to x = x − y.

**\*= : Multiply and assign**

$x *= y$

x's value is equal to 91. It is equivalent to x = x * y.

**/= : Divide and assign**

$x /= y$

x's value is equal to 1.8571428571428572. It is equivalent to x = x / y.

**\*\*= : Exponent and Assign**

$x **= y$

x's value is equal to 62748517. It is equivalent to x = x ** y.

**//= : Floor Division and Assign**

$x //= y$

x's value is equal to 1. It is equivalent to x = x // y.

**%= : Modulus and Assign**

**x %= y**

x's value is equal to 6. It is equivalent to x = x % y.

## *Multiple Usage of Some Operators*

Also, some operators may behave differently depending on how you use them or what values you use together with them. For example:

**z = "sample" + "statement"**

As you can see, the statement tried to add two strings. In other programming languages, that kind of statement will return an error since their (+) operator is dedicated for addition of numbers only. In Python, it will perform string concatenation that will append the second string to the first. Hence, the value of variable z will become "samplestatement".

On the other hand, you can use the (-) subtraction operator as unary operators. To denote that a variable or number is negative, you can place the subtraction operator before it. For example:

**z = 1 - -1**

The result will be 2 since 1 minus negative 1 is 2.

The addition operator acts as a unary operator for other languages; however, it behaves differently in Python. In some language, an expression like this: +(-1), will be treated as positive 1. In Python, it will be treated as +1(-1), and if you evaluate that, you will still get negative 1.

To perform a unary positive, you can do this instead:

**--1**

In that example, Python will read it as −(-1) or -1 * -1 and it will return a positive 1.

# Chapter 5: Basic Operators – Part 2

Operators seem to be such a big topic, right? You will be working with them all
the time when programming in Python. Once you master or just memorize them
all, your overall programming skills will improve since most programming
languages have operators that work just like the ones in Python.

And just like a restaurant manager, you would not want to let your chef serve
food with only unprocessed ingredients all the time. Not everybody wants salads
for their dinner.

## *Comparison*

Aside from performing arithmetic operations and storing values to variables,
Python can also allow you to let the computer compare expressions. For example,
you can ask your computer if 10 is greater than 20. Since 10 is greater than 20, it
will reply with True – meaning the statement you said was correct. If you have
compared 20 is greater than 10 instead, it will return a reply that says False.

### == : Is Equal

**z = x == y**

z's value is equal to FALSE.

### != : Is Not Equal

**z = x != y**

z's value is equal to True.

### > : Is Greater Than

**z = x > y**

z's value is equal to True.

### < : Is Less Than

**z = x < y**

z's value is equal to FALSE.

### >= : Is Greater Than or Equal

**z = x >= y**

z's value is equal to True.

### <= : Is Less Than or Equal

**z = x <= y**

z's value is equal to FALSE.

Note that the last two operators are unlike the combined arithmetic and simple assignment operator.

## *Logical*

Aside from arithmetic and comparison operations, the computer is capable of logical operations, too. Even simple circuitry can do that, but that is another story to tell.

Anyway, do you remember your logic class where your professor talked about truth tables, premises, and propositions? Your computer can understand all of that. Below are the operators you can use to perform logic in Python. In the examples in the list, a is equal to True and b is equal to False.

**and : Logical Conjunction AND. It will return only True both the propositions or variable besides it is True. It will return False if any or both the propositions are False.**

**w = a and a**

**x = a and b**

**y = b and a**

**z = b and b**

w is equal to True, x is equal to False, y is equal to False, and z is    equal to False.

**or  : Logical Disjunction OR. It will return True if any or both of the proposition or variable beside it is True. It will return False if both the propositions are False.**

**w = a or a**

**x = a or b**

**y = b or a**

**z = b or b**

w is equal to True, x is equal to True, y is equal to True, and z is    equal to False.

17

not : Logical Negation NOT. Any Truth value besides it will be negated. If True is negated, the computer will reply with a False. If False is negated, the computer will reply with a True.

**w = not a**

**x = not b**

w is equal to False and x is equal to True.

If you want to perform Logical NAND, you can use Logic Negation NOT and Logical Conjunction AND. For example:

**w = not (a and a)**

**x = not (a and b)**

**y = not (b and a)**

**z = not (b and b)**

w is equal to False, x is equal to True, y is equal to True, and z is equal to True.

If you want to perform Logical NOR, you can use Logic Negation NOT and Logical Disjunction OR. For example:

**w = not (a or a)**

**x = not (a or b)**

**y = not (b or a)**

**z = not (b or b)**

w is equal to False, x is equal to False, y is equal to False, and z is equal to True.

You can perform other logical operations that do not have Python operators by using conditional statements, which will be discussed later in this book.

## *Order of Precedence*

In case that your statement contains multiple types or instances of operators, Python will evaluate it according to precedence of the operators, which is similar to the PEMDAS rule in Mathematics. It will evaluate the operators with the highest precedence to the lowest. For example:

**z = 2 + 10 / 10**

Instead of adding 2 and 10 first then dividing the sum by 10, Python will divide 10 by 10 first then add 2 to the quotient instead since division has a higher precedence than subtraction. So, instead of getting 1.2, you will get 3.0. In case that it confuses you, imagine that Python secretly adds parentheses to the expression. The sample above is the same as:

**z = 2 + (10 / 10)**

If two operators with the same level of precedence exist in one statement, Python will evaluate the first operator that appears from the left. For example:

**z = 10 / 10 * 2**

The value of variable z will be 2.

Take note that any expressions inside parentheses or nested deeper in parentheses will have higher precedence than those expressions outside the parentheses. For example:

**z = 2 / ((1 + 1) * (2 − 4))**

Even though the division operator came first and has higher precedence than addition and subtraction, Python evaluated the ones inside the parentheses first and evaluated the division operation last. So, it added 1 and 1, subtracted 4 from 2, multiplied the sum and difference of the two previous operations, and then divided the product from 2. The value of variable z became -0.5.

Below is a reference for the precedence of the operations. The list is sorted from operations with high precedence to operators with low precedence.

- ➤ **Exponents**
- ➤ **Unary**
- ➤ **Multiplication, Division, Modulo, and Floor Division**
- ➤ **Addition, and Subtraction**
- ➤ **Bitwise**
- ➤ **Comparison**
- ➤ **Assignment**
- ➤ **Identity**
- ➤ **Membership**
- ➤ **Logical**

## *Truth Values*

The values True and False are called truth values – or sometimes called Boolean data values. The value True is equal to 1 and the value False is equal to 0. That means that you can treat or use 1 as the truth value True and 0 as the truth value False. Try comparing those two values in your interpreter. Code the following:

**True == 1**

**False == 0**

The interpreter will return a value of True – meaning, you can interchange them in case a situation arises. However, it is advisable that that you use them like that sparingly.

Another thing you should remember is that the value True and False are case sensitive. True != TRUE or False != false. Aside from that, True and False are Python keywords. You cannot create variables named after them.

You might be wondering about the use of truth values in programming. The answer is, you can use them to control your programs using conditional or flow control tools. With them, you can make your program execute statements when a certain condition arises. And that will be discussed on the next chapter.

# Chapter 6: Functions, Flow Control, and User Input

With statements, you have learned to tell instructions to the computer using Pythons. As of now, all you know is how to assign variables and manipulate expressions. And the only command you know is print. Do you think you can make a decent program with those alone? Maybe, but you do not need to rack your brains thinking of one.

In this chapter, you will learn about functions and flow control. This time, you will need to leave the interpreter or Interactive mode. Open your source code editor since you will be programming blocks of codes during this section.

## *Functions*

Statements are like sentences in a book or steps in a recipe. On the other hand, functions are like paragraphs or a recipe in a recipe book. Functions are blocks of code with multiple statements that will perform a specific goal or goals when executed. Below is an example:

**def recipe1():**

> **print("Fried Fish Recipe")**
>
> **print("Ingredients:")**
>
> **print("Fish")**
>
> **print("Salt")**
>
> **print("Steps:")**
>
> **print("1. Rub salt on fish.")**
>
> **print("2. Fry fish.")**
>
> **print("3. Serve.")**

The function's purpose is to print the recipe for Fried Fish. To create a function, you will need to type the keyword def (for define) then the name of the function. In the example, the name of the function is recipe1. The parentheses are important to be present there. It has its purpose, but for now, leave it alone.

After the parentheses, a colon was placed. The colon signifies that a code block will be under the function.

To include statements inside that code block, you must indent it. In the example, one indentation or tab was used. To prevent encountering errors, make sure that all the statements are aligned and have the same number of indentations.

To end the code block for the function, all you need is to type a statement that has the same indentation level of the function declaration.

By the way, all the statements inside a function code block will not be executed until the function is called or invoked. To invoke the function, all you need is to call it using its name. To invoke the function recipe1, type this:

**recipe1()**

And that is how simple functions work.

## Flow Control

It is sad that only one recipe can be displayed by the sample function. It would be great if your program can display more recipes. And letting the user choose the recipe that they want to be displayed on the program would be cool. But how can you do that?

You can do that by using flow control tools in Python. With them, you can direct your program to do something if certain conditions are met. In the case of the recipe listing program, you can apply flow control and let them see the recipes by requesting it.

## If Statement

The simplest control flow tool you can use for this type of project is the if statement. Have you been wondering about truth values? Now, you can use them with if statements.

An *if statement* is like a program roadblock. If the current condition of your program satisfies its requirements, then it will let it access the block of statements within it. It is like a function with no names, and instead of being invoked to work, it needs you to satisfy the conditions set to it. For example:

**a = 2**

**if a == 2:**

> **print("You satisfied the condition!")**

> **print("This is another statement that will be executed!")**

**if a == (1 + 1):**

> **print("You satisfied the condition again!")**

> **print("I will display the recipe for Fried Fish!")**

> **recipe1()**

If you will translate the first if statement in English, it will mean that: if variable a is equals to 2, then print the sentence inside the parentheses. Another way to translate it is: if the comparison between variable a and the number 2 returns True, then print the sentence inside the parentheses.

As you can see, the colon is there and the statements below the if statement are indented, too. It really is like a function.

## *User Input*

You can now control the flow of your program and create functions. Now, about the recipe program, how can the user choose the recipe he wants to view? That can be done by using the input() command. You can use it like this:

**a = input("Type your choice here and press enter: ")**

Once Python executes that line, it will stop executing statements. And provide a prompt that says "Type your choice here: ". During that moment, the user will be given a chance to type something in the program. If the user press enter, Python will store and assign the characters the user typed on the program to variable a. Once that process is done, Python will resume executing the statements after the input statement.

In some cases, programmers use the input command to pause the program and wait for the user to press enter. You can do that by just placing input() on a line.

With that, you can make a program that can capture user input and can change its flow whenever it gets the right values from the user. You can create a recipe program that allows users to choose the recipe they want. Here is the code. Analyze it. And use the things you have learned to improve it. Good luck.

**print("Enter the number of the recipe you want to read.")**

**print("1 - Fried Fish")**

**print("2 - Fried Egg")**

**print("Enter any character to Exit")**

**choice = input("Type a Number and Press Enter: ")**

**if choice == "1":**

    **print("Fried Fish Recipe")**

    **print("Ingredients:")**

    **print("Fish")**

```python
print("Salt")

print("Steps:")

print("1. Rub salt on fish.")

print("2. Fry fish.")

print("3. Serve.")

pause = input("Press enter when you are done reading.")


if choice == "2":

    print("Fried Egg Recipe")

    print("Ingredients:")

    print("Egg")

    print("Salt")

    print("Steps:")

    print("1. Fry egg.")

    print("2. Sprinkle Salt.")

    print("3. Serve.")

    pause = input("Press enter when you are done reading.")
```

# Conclusion

Thank you again for purchasing this book!

I hope this book was able to help you to learn the basics of Python programming.

The next step is to learn more about Python! You should have expected that coming.

Kidding aside, with the current knowledge you have in Python programming, you can make any programs like that with ease. But of course, there are still lots of things you need to learn about the language such as loops, classes, and etcetera.

Finally, if you enjoyed this book, please take the time to share your thoughts and post a review on Amazon. We do our best to reach out to readers and provide the best value we can. Your positive review will help us achieve that. It'd be greatly appreciated!

Thank you and good luck!

# Book 2
# CSS Programming Professional Made Easy

By Sam Key

*Expert CSS Programming Language Success in a Day for any Computer User!*

**Programming Box Set #52: Python Programming Professional Made Easy & CSS Programming Professional Made Easy**

# Table of Contents

# Introduction

I want to thank you and congratulate you for purchasing the book, "Professional CSS Programming Made Easy: Expert CSS Programming Language Success In A Day for any Computer User!".

This book contains proven steps and strategies on how to effectively apply CSS style rules in making your webpages more appealing to your readers. In this book, the different aspects of CSS programming are discussed in simple language to make it easy for you to understand even if you have no previous experience in programming. In no time, you can start creating your own CSS style rules!

Thanks again for purchasing this book, I hope you enjoy it!

# Chapter 1: What is CSS?

CSS is short for Cascading Style Sheets which is a simple design language that is meant to streamline the enhancement of web page presentations. Basically, through CSS, you will be able to manage how a web page looks and feels. When you use CSS, you will be able to control the background color or image in the web page, the color of the texts, the style of the font, the size of the columns, the column layout, the spacing in between paragraphs and a whole lot more of design effects.

Even though CSS is quite simple to understand, it can provide you with great control of how an HTML document is presented. People who study CSS often study other markup languages such as XHTML or HTML.

What are the advantages of CSS?

- CSS will allow you to save time. After you have written a CSS code once, you can then use the same sheet in various web pages. You can create a style for each web page element and then use it to as many HTML pages as you desire in the future.

- Your web pages will load faster. If you will use CSS in your web pages, you no longer have to write an HTML tag attribute all the time. You simple create 1 CSS rule of a tag and then use it for all the incidences of that specific tag. When you use less HTML codes, it translates to faster download speed.

- Your web pages become easier to maintain. If you wish to create a global change in your website, all you need to do is adjust the style and then all the elements included in your different web pages will be automatically adjusted.

- You will be able to enjoy better styles compared to HTML. The style attributes available for HTML codes are lesser compared to what you can work with when you use CSS. This means that you will be able to create top quality styles for your web pages.

- You will have multiple device compatibility. With CSS, you will be allowed to use content that can be optimized for different types of device. Even when you use the same HTML document, you can present the website in various versions for different devices such as mobile phones, tablets, desktop and even printing.

- You will be able to adopt web standards that are recognized globally. More and more people are losing interest in using HTML attributes and have started to recommend the use of CSS.

- You get to future-proof. By using CSS in your web pages now, you can also ensure that they will have compatibility with future browsers.

Creation and Maintenance of CSS

Only a small group of people within the World Wide Web Consortium (W3C) referred to as the CSS Working Group is allowed to create and maintain CSS. This group generates the CSS specifications which are then submitted to the W3C members for discussion and ratification. Only ratified specifications are given the recommendation signal by the W3C. You need to note that they are referred to as recommendations since the W3C cannot really dictate how the language is to be actually implementation. The software the implement the CSS language is created by independent organizations and companies.

Note: If you wish to know, yes, the W3C is the group that provides the recommendations on how the Internet should work and how it should progress.

Different CSS Versions

The W3C released CSS1 or Cascading Style Sheets Level 1was released as a recommendation in 1996. The recommendation included a description of the CSS together with a basic visual formatting model that can be used for every HTML tag.

In May 1998, the W3C released the recommendation for CSS2 or Cascading Style Sheets Level 2 which included further information that builds on CSS1. CSS2 added support for style sheets for specific media such as aural devices, printers, element tables and positioning and downloadable fonts.

# Chapter 2: Various Types of CSS Selectors

A CSS is composed of different style rules that are translated by the browser for them to be applied to the specific elements in your web page. A style rule is further composed of 3 parts: selector, property and value. A selector is the HTML tag wherein the style rule will be applied. Examples include <table> or <h1>. A property is the specific attribute type that an HTML tag has. In simple terms, you could say that each HTML attribute is ultimately translated to a CSS property. Examples of properties include border or color. Values, on the other hand, are directly assigned to the properties. For instance, for the color property, you can assign a value of #000000 or black.

One way to write a CSS Style Rule Syntax is: Selector (property: value)

Ex. You can write the syntax rule for a table border as: table (border: 2px solid #C00;). The selector in this example is table while the property is the border. The specific value given for the property is 2px solid #C00.

In this chapter, we will be talking about the different kinds of selectors.

Type Selector

The selector in the example given above (table) is categorized under the Type Selector. Another example of a type Selector is "level 1 heading" or "h1). We can write a CSS Style Rule Syntax as: h1 (color: #36CFFF;). The selector in this example is h1 while the property is the color. The specific value given for the property is #36CFF.

Universal Selector

This is designated by an asterisk (*) which means that the style rule syntax that you want to create will be applied to all elements in your webpage and not only to specific elements.

Example: *(color: #FFFFFF;). This style rule means that you want all of the elements (including fonts, borders, etc.) in your webpage to be white.

Descendant Selector

You use the descendant selector when you wish to apply a certain style rule for a specific element that lies within a specific element.

Example: ul em (color:#FFFFFF;), the value #FFFFFF (white) will only be applied to the property (color) if the selector/property <em> lies within the selector <ul>.

Class Selector

Using the Class Selector, you will be able to define a specific style rule that can be applied based on the specific class attribute of elements. This means that all of the elements that have that specific class attributed will have the same formatting as specified in the style rule.

Example 1: .white (color: #FFFFFF;). Here the class attribute is "white" and it means that the color "white" will be applied to all of the elements given the class attribute "white" in your document.

Example 2: h1.white (color: #FFFFFF;). This style rule is more specific. The class attribute is still "white" and the style rule will be applied to the elements given the class attribute "white" but ONLY if they are ALSO an <h1> or "level 1 heading" element.

You can actually give one or more class selectors for each element. For example, you can give the class selectors "center" and "bold" to a paragraph <p> by writing it as <p class="center,bold">.

ID Selector

You use an ID selector to create a style rule that is based on the specific ID attribute of the element. This means that all of the elements that have that specific ID will have the same format as defined in the style rule.

Example 1: #white (color: #FFFFFF;). The ID assigned here is "white" and the style rule means that all elements with the "white" ID attribute will be rendered black in your document.

Example 2: h1#white (color: #FFFFFF;). This is more specific because it means that the style rule will only be applied to elements with the ID attribute "white" ONLY IF they are a level 1 heading element.

The ID selectors are ideally used as foundations for descendant selectors. Example: #white h3 (color: #FFFFFF;). The style rule dictates that all level 3 headings located in the different pages of your website will be displayed in white color ONLY IF those level 3 headings are within tags that have an ID attribute of "white".

33

Child Selector

The Child Selector is quite similar to the Descendant Selector except that they have different functionalities.

Example: body > p (color: #FFFFFF;). The style rule states that a paragraph will be rendered in white if it is a direct child of the <body> element. If the paragraph is within other elements such as <td> or <div>, the style rule will not apply to it.

Attribute Selector

You can apply specific styles to your webpage elements that have specific attributes.

Example: input(type="text"](color: #FFFFFF;).

One benefit of the above example is that the specified color in the style rule will only affect your desired text field and will not affect the <input type="submit"/>.

You need to keep the following rules in mind when using attribute selectors:

•    p[lang]. All elements of the paragraph that has a "lang" attribute will be selected.

•    p[lang="fr"]. All elements of the paragraph that has a "lang" attribute AND the value "fr" in the "lang" attribute will be selected. Note that the value should exactly be "fr".

•    p[lang~="fr"]. All elements of the paragraph that has a "lang" attribute AND CONTAINS the value "fr" in the "lang" attribute will be selected.

•    p[lang |="ne"]. All elements of the paragraph that has a "lang" attribute AND CONTAINS value that is EITHER exactly "en" or starts with "en-" in the "lang" attribute will be selected.

Multiple Style Rules

It is possible for you to create multiple style rules for one specific element. The style rules can be defined in such a way that different properties are combined into a single block and specific values are assigned to each property.

Example 1:

h1(color: #35C; font-weight: bold; letter-spacing: .5em; margin-bottom: 1em; text-transform: uppercase;)

You will note that the properties and their corresponding values are separated from other property/value pairs by using a semi-colon. You can opt to write the combine style rules as a single line similar to the example above or as multiple lines for better readability. The example below is just the same as Example 1:

Example 2:

h1 (

color: #35C;

font-weight: bold;

letter-spacing: .5em;

margin-bottom: 1em;

text-transform: uppercase;

)

How to Group Selectors

You can actually apply one single style to different selectors. All you really need to do is write all the selectors at the start of your style rule but make sure that they are separated by a comma. The examples above both pertain to the selector or property "level 1 heading". If you want to apply the same style rule to "level 2 heading" and "level 3 heading", you can include h2 and h3 in the first line, as follows:

Example:

h1, h2, h3 (

color: #35C;

font-weight: bold;

letter-spacing: .5em;

margin-bottom: 1em;

text-transform: uppercase;

)

Note that the sequence of the selector element is not relevant. You can write it as h3,h2,h1 and the style rule will exactly be the same. It means that the specified style rules will still be applied to all the elements of the selectors.

It is also possible to create a style rule that combines different class selectors.

Example:

#supplement, #footer, #content (

position: absolute;

left: 520px;

width: 210px;

)

# Chapter 3: Methods of Associating Styles

There are actually 4 methods of associating styles within an HTML document – Embedded CSS, Inline CSS, External CSS and Imported CSS. But the two most frequently used are Inline CSS and External CSS.

Embedded CSS

This method uses the <style> element wherein the tags are positioned within the <head>...</head> tags. All elements that exist within your document will be affected by a rule that has been written using this syntax. The generic syntax is as follows:

<head>

<style type="text/css" media="...">

Style Rules

. . . . . . . . . . .

</style>

</head>

The following attributes that are connected to the <style> element are as follows:

•       Type with value "text/css". This attribute indicates the style sheet language as a content-type (MIME type). You need to note that this attribute is always required.

•       Media with values as "screen", "tty", "tv", "projection", "handheld", "print", "braille", "aural" or "all". This attribute indicates what kind of device the webpage will be shown. This attribute is only optional and it always has "all" as a default value.

 Example:

<head>

<style type="text/css" media="screen">

h2(

color: #38C;

)

</style>

</head>

## Inline CSS

This method uses the style attribute of a specific HTML element in defining the style rule. This means that the style rule will only be applied to the specific HTML element ONLY. The generic syntax is as follows: <element style=". . .style rules. . . .">

Only one attribute is connected to the <style> attribute and it is as follows:

• Style with value "style rules". The value that you will specify for the style attribute is basically a combination of various style declarations. You should use a semicolon to separate the different style declarations.

Example:

<h2 style ="color:#000;">. This is inline CSS </h2>

## External CSS

This method uses the <link> element in defining the style rule. You can use it to add external style sheets within your webpage. The external style sheet that you will add will have a different text file that has the extension .css. All the style rules that you want to apply to your webpage elements will be added inside the external text file and then you can append the text file in any of your web pages by creating the <link> element. The general syntax that you will be using will be:

<head>

<link type="text/css" href=" . . ." media=" . . ." />

</head>

The following attributes that are connected with the <style> elements are as follows:

• Type with the value "text/css". This indicates that you are using a MIME type or a content type for your style sheet language. Note that you are always required to use this attribute.

•       Href with value "URL". This attribute will indicate the specific style sheet file that contains your style rules. Again, you are also always required to use this attribute.

•       Media with value "screen", "tty", "tv", "projection", "handheld", "print", "braille", "aural" or "all". This attribute indicates the specific media device that you will use to display the document. This attribute is only optional and it has a default value of "all".

Example wherein the style sheet file is named as docstyle.css:

h2, h3 (

color: #38C;

font-weight: bold;

letter-spacing: .5em;

margin-bottom: 2em;

text-transform: uppercase;

)

Then you can add your style sheet file "docstyle.css" in your webpage by adding these rules:

<head>

<link type="text/css" href="docstyle.css" media="all" />

</head>


Imported CSS

This method which uses the @import rule is the same as the <link> element because it is used to import an external style sheet file to your webpage. The generic syntax of this method is as follows:

<head>

<@import "URL";

</head>


Here is another alternative syntax that you can use:

```
<head>
<@import url ("URL");
</head>
```

Example:

```
<head>
@import "docstyle.css"'
</head>
```

How to Override CSS Style Rules

The following can override the style rules that you have created using the above four methods:

•       An inline style sheet is given the number one priority. This means that an inline style sheet will always supersede a rule that has been written with a <style>...</style> tag or a rule that has been defined in an external stylesheet file.

•       A rule that has been written with a <style>...</style> tag will always supersede a style rule that has been defined in an external stylesheet file.

•       The rules that you define within an external stylesheet file is always given the lowest priority. This means that any rules defined within the external file will only be applied if the 2 rules above aren't valid.

How to Handle an Old Browser:

Currently, there are a lot of old browsers that are not yet capable of supporting CSS. When you are working with these kind of browsers, you need to write your embedded CSS within the HTML document. Here is an example on how you can embed CSS in an old browser:

```
<style type="text/css">
<!—
Body, td (
    Color: red;
)
```

-->

</style>

How to Add a CSS Comment

In case it is necessary for you to include an additional comment within the style sheet block, you can easily do this by writing your comment within /*....this is a comment in style sheet....*/. The /*....*/ method used in C++ and C programming languages can also be used in adding comments in a multi-line block.

Example:

/* This is an external style sheet file */

h3, h2, h1 (

color: #38C;

font-weight: bold;

letter-spacing: .5em;

margin-bottom: 2em;

text-transform: uppercase;

)

/* end of style rules. */

# Chapter 4: Measurement Units

There are several measurements that CSS can support. These include absolute units like inch, centimeter, points, etc. They also include relative measures like em unit and percentage. These values are important when you want to specify the different measurements you want to include in your style rule. Example:

border="2px solid black".

Here are the most common measurements that you will use in creating CSS style rules:

| Unit of Measure | Description | Example |
|---|---|---|
| % | Indicates measurements as a percentage in relation to another value which is normally an enclosing element | p {font-size: 12pt; line-height: 150%;} |
| cm | Indicates measurements in centimeter | div {margin-bottom: 1.5cm;} |
| em | A relative number used in measuring font height using em spaces. One em unit is equal to the size of a particular font. This means, if you want a certain font to have a size of 10pt, one "em" unit is equal to 10pt and 3em is equal to 30pt. | p {letter-spacing: 6em;} |
| ex | A number used to define a measurement in relation to the x-height of a font. The x-height is defined by the height of letter x in lowercase in any given font. | p {font-size: 20pt; line-height: 2ex;} |
| in | Indicates measurements in inches | p {word-spacing: .12in;} |
| mm | Indicates measurements in millimeter | p {word-spacing: 12mm;} |
| pc | Indicates measurements in picas. One pica is equal to 12 points. This | p {font-size: 18pc;} |

|  | means that there are six picas in one inch. |  |
|---|---|---|
| pt | Indicates measurements in points. One point is equal to 1/72 of one inch. | body {font-size: 20pt;} |
| px | Indicates measurements in screen pixel | p {padding: 32px;} |

# Chapter 5: Style Rules Using Colors

A color in CSS style rules is indicated by color values. Normally, the color values are used to define the color of either the background of an element or its foreground (that is, its text). You can also utilize colors to change how your borders and other aesthetic effects look.

Color values in CSS rules can be specified using the following formats:

•	Hex code using the syntax #RRGGBB. Example: p {color: #FFFF00;}. The six digits represent one specific color wherein RR represents the value for red, GG the value for green and BB the value for blue. You can get the hexadecimal values of different colors from graphics software such as Jasc Paintshop Pro and Adobe Photoshop. You can also use the Advanced Paint Brush to get the hexadecimal values. You need to note that the six digits should always be preceded by the hash or pound sign (#).

•	Short hex code using the syntax #RGB. Example: p {color: #7A6;}. This is the shorter version of the hexadecimal value. You can also get them from Jasc Paintshop Pro, Adobe Photoshop or Advanced Paint Brush.

•	RGB % using the syntax rgb (rrr%, ggg%, bbb%). Example: p{color: rgb (40%, 50%, 40%);}. This format is actually advisable to use because not all browsers support this type of format.

•	RGB Absolute using the syntax rgb (rrr,ggg, bbb). Example: p {color: rgb (255,0,0);}

•	Keyword using the syntax black, aqua, etc. Example: p {color: red;}

# Chapter 6: How to Set Backgrounds

What you will learn in this chapter includes how to define the background of the different elements in your web page. You can use any of the following background properties for specific elements in your webpage:

• You can use the background color property to define the background color of your element.

• You can use the background image property to define the background image of your element.

• You can use the background repeat property to control whether your background image will be repeated or not.

• You can use the background position property to control the position of the background image.

• You can use the background attachment property to define whether your image is fixed or will scroll with the rest of the webpage.

• You can use the background property to combine the above properties into one style rule.

Background Color

Here is a sample of how you can define the background color:

RED

This will result in RED.

Background Image

Here is a sample of how you can define the background image:

<table style="background-image:url (/images/pattern1.jpg);">

<tr><td>

The table now has an image in the background.

```
</td></tr>
```

```
</table>
```

How to Repeat a Background Image

In case your image is small, you can opt to repeat your background image. Otherwise, you can simple utilize the "no-repeat" value in the background-repeat property if you do not wish to have your background image repeated. This means that your image will only be displayed once. Note that "repeat value" is the default value in the background-repeat property.

Example:

```
<table style="background-image:url (/images/pattern2.jpg);

            background-repeat: repeat;">
```

```
<tr><td>
```

The background image in this table will be repeated several times.

```
</td></tr>
```

```
</table>
```

Here is a sample rule if you want the background image to be repeated vertically:

```
<table style="background-image:url (/images/pattern2.jpg);

            background-repeat: repeat-y;">
```

```
<tr><td>
```

The background image in this table will be repeated vertically.

```
</td></tr>
```

```
</table>
```

Here is a sample rule if you want the background image to be repeated horizontally:

```
<table style="background-image:url (/images/pattern2.jpg);

            background-repeat: repeat-x;">
```

<tr><td>

The background image in this table will be repeated horizontally.

</td></tr>

</table>


How to Set the Position of the Background Image

Here is a sample of how you can define the position of a background image at 150 pixels from the left side:

<table style="background-image: url (/images/pattern2.jpg);

Background-position:150px;">

<tr><td>

The position of the background is now 150 pixels from the left side.

</td></tr>

</table>


Here is a sample of how you can define the position of a background image at 300 pixels from the top and 150 pixels from the left side:

<table style="background-image: url (/images/pattern2.jpg);

Background-position:150px 300px;">

<tr><td>

The position of the background is now 300 pixels from the top and 150 pixels from the left side.

</td></tr>

</table>


How to Define the Background Attachment

The background attachment indicates whether the background image that you have set is fixed in its place or scrolls when you move the webpage.

Here is an example on how to write a style rule with a background image that is fixed:

<p style="background-image:url (/images/pattern2.jpg);

        Background-attachment:fixed;">

The paragraph now has a background image that is fixed.

</p>


Here is an example on how to write a style rule with a background image that scrolls with the webpage:

<p style="background-image:url (/images/pattern2.jpg);

        Background-attachment:scroll;">

The paragraph now has a background image that scrolls with the webpage.

</p>


How to Use the Shorthand Property

You can actually utilize the background property in order to define all of the background properties all at the same time.

Example:

<p style="background:url (/images/pattern2.jpg) repeat scroll;">

The background image of this paragraph has a scroll and repeated properties.

</p>

# Chapter 7: How to Set Font Properties

What you will learn in this chapter includes how to define the following font properties to a specific element in your webpage:

• You can use the font family property to adjust the face of your selected font.

• You can use the font style property to make your fonts either oblique or italic.

• You can use the font variant property to include the "small caps" effect in your fonts.

• You can use the font weight property to decrease or increase how light or bold your fonts are displayed.

• You can use the font size property to decrease or increase the sizes of your fonts.

• You can use the font property to define a combination of the font properties above.


How to Define the Font Family

Here is an example on how you can define the font family of a specific element. As value of the property, you can use any of the font family names available:

This message is displayed either in calibri, arial or the default serif font. It will depend on the existing fonts in your system.

How to Define the Font Style

Here is an example on how you can define the font style of a specific element. The values that you can use are oblique, italic or normal.

This message is displayed in oblique style.

How to Define the Font Variant

Here is an example on how you define the font variant of a specific element. The values that you can use are small-caps or normal.

This message is displayed in normal font variant.

How to Define the Font Weight

Here is an example on how you can define the font weight of a specific element. With this property, you will be able to define how bold you want your fonts to be. The values that you can use are bold, normal, lighter, bolder, 100, 200, 300, 400, 500, 600, 700, 800, and 900.

The font is displayed with normal font weight.

The font is displayed with lighter font weight.

The font is displayed with 800 font weight.

How to Define the Font Size

Here is an example on how you can define the font size of a specific element. With this property, you will be able to control the font sizes in your webpage. The values that you can use include small, medium, large, x-small, xx-small, xx-large, x-large, larger, smaller, size in % or size in pixels.

The font is displayed with 18 pixels font size.

The font is displayed with large font size.

The font is displayed with larger font size.

How to Define the Font Size Adjust

Here is an example on how you can define the font size adjust of a specific element. With this property, you will be able to adjust the x-height in order to make the legibility of your fonts better. The values that you can use include any number.

The font is displayed with 0.75 font size adjust value.

How to Define the Font Stretch

Here is an example on how you can define the font stretch of a specific element. With this property, you can allow the computer of your webpage readers to have a condensed or expanded version of the font you have defined in your elements. The values that you can use include normal, narrower, wider, condensed, extra-condensed, semi-condensed, ultra-condensed, semi-expanded, ultra-expanded, expanded and extra-expanded

If this does not seem to work, it is probably that the computer you are using does not have an expanded or condensed version of the font that was used.

How to Use the Shorthand Property

You can utilize the font property to define the font properties all at the same time.

Example:

## Programming Box Set #52: Python Programming Professional Made Easy & CSS Programming Professional Made Easy

```
<p style="font:oblique normal bolder 20px calibri;">
```

This applies all of the defined properties on the text all at the same time.

```
</p>
```

# Conclusion

Thank you again for purchasing this book!

I hope this book was able to help you to understand the basic CSS styling rules.

The next step is to apply what you have just learned in your own webpage.

Finally, if you enjoyed this book, please take the time to share your thoughts and post a review on Amazon. We do our best to reach out to readers and provide the best value we can. Your positive review will help us achieve that. It'd be greatly appreciated!

Thank you and good luck!

## Check Out My Other Books

Below you'll find some of my other popular books that are popular on Amazon and Kindle as well. Simply click on the links below to check them out. Alternatively, you can visit my author page on Amazon to see other work done by me.

Android Programming in a Day

Python Programming in a Day

C Programming Success in a Day

C Programming Professional Made Easy

JavaScript Programming Made Easy

PHP Programming Professional Made Easy

C ++ Programming Success in a Day

Windows 8 Tips for Beginners

HTML Professional Programming Made Easy

If the links do not work, for whatever reason, you can simply search for these titles on the Amazon website to find them.